God I need to talk to You about Anger

Michael Newman

CONCORDIA PUBLISHING HOUSE · SAINT LOUIS

Copyright © 2013 Concordia Publishing House
3558 S. Jefferson Avenue, St. Louis, MO 63118-3968
1-800-325-3040 · www.cph.org

Written by Michael Newman

Manufactured in the United States of America

1 2 3 4 5 6 7 8 9 10 22 21 20 19 18 17 16 15 14 13

Table of CONTENTS

A note to the reader: Some of the details in these prayers may not reflect your unique situation. Therefore, we encourage you to adapt them where appropriate to fit your circumstances and spiritual needs.

Introduction

This can be an ugly world, and there's a lot in it that warrants our anger. Anger, in itself, isn't bad. In fact, anger can spark good things; it might launch a movement to end something harmful, such as pollution or child abuse. It can be constructive and help to fix something that is within our realm to fix.

Emotions are not bad. Our God created us to have them, and the Bible is packed with examples of God's feelings, of Jesus' emotions. But emotion is a problem when it is excessive, unwarranted, or harmful. This happens, for example, when anger damages relationships, jeopardizes employment, or contributes to other harmful situations or circumstances. Regardless of how justified we feel in our anger toward another driver, a clerk, or an umpire, throwing a temper tantrum never helps anything.

The causes of anger range from physical and mental illness to learned patterns of behavior and bad habits. It's important to identify the causes of harmful anger and to recognize the triggers so the outbursts can be controlled and diagnosed, if need be. Possible mental and physical causes of angry outbursts are well beyond the scope and intent of this little prayer book. In many cases, it's wise to seek the aid of a medical professional or counselor to identify the causes of angry outbursts and work toward overcoming them.

But a bad habit, now that's something we can work on.

If angry outbursts are simply the result of habit or behavioral patterns, then intentional awareness and prayer may help us change our responses and work toward repairing damage caused to relationships. When we recognize our behaviors as choices we make, we can summon the courage and strength to apologize and develop new habits.

Our hope is that this little book helps with that. But ultimately, our intention is that these prayers will be reminders and assurances that Jesus offers forgiveness. For everything. He forgives us, and because of that, we can learn to forgive others and ourselves.

Blowing Up

Dear God,

I'm talking to You because I think I've driven away too many people in my life because of my anger. I can't help it. When I feel wronged and betrayed, when I get frustrated and tired, I can't help but blow up. One "last straw" is added to the pile, and I lose it. I lash out.

Sometimes it seems to come out of nowhere. Someone pushes the right button, and I erupt like a volcano. There is something inside of me that keeps my anger very close to the surface. I don't like it. I don't like what it does to me. I don't like how it hurts the people around me.

Help me, God. I know I can't help myself. This is something out of my control.

When I settle down physically and calm down emotionally, I understand what I've done and feel terrible about it. But by that time it seems too late. People don't trust me. They've even become afraid of me. I'd be afraid of me too. I can be pretty scary when I'm mad.

So I'm asking You to step in. I need You to save me from the damage I've done. I need You to save me from plunging into rage and outbursts. I know You came to give me peace. Please rescue me and guide me, dear Savior.

Something to think about

[Jesus said,] "Peace I leave with you; My peace I give to you. Not as the world gives do I give to you. Let not your hearts be troubled, neither let them be afraid."

John 14:27

Injustice

Dear God,

Thank You for listening to me as I come to You in my failure and sin. My anger hangs in my life like a dark and stormy cloud. I feel unworthy to come to You at all. But I know You love me. I know You sent Your Son, Jesus, to forgive me and give me new life. You are my hope.

I need hope because I feel like my emotions are so often on the edge of losing control. I believe what triggers my anger most is betrayal. When a co-worker doesn't keep his word or when one of my kids breaks a clear and agreed-upon rule, I can't understand it. When I confront them about it and receive a response of denial or apathy or attitude, I feel the blood rush to my head. One more nudge in the wrong direction and I'm exploding.

But at the root of all this is injustice. I know I'm right about the issues. I'm not being unfair or unclear. We agreed to certain standards and rules. All I expect is loyalty and integrity. But, instead, I'm slapped in the face with disloyalty and carelessness. It hurts. It's wrong. It's not fair.

Then I become the bad guy. I'm the angry one who causes trouble. But it didn't start with me!

I don't know how to end this vicious cycle. I can't stop caring about what is right. But I can't keep losing control either. You showed that You are the Prince of Peace through Your Son, Jesus. Please send that peace to me.

Something to think about

You know the message God sent to the people of Israel, announcing the good news of peace through Jesus Christ, who is Lord of all.

Acts 10:36 NIV

Being Still

Dear God,

I praise You and thank You for hearing me and directing me to Your Word. I looked at Psalm 37 today. In verse 8, I saw these wise words: "Refrain from anger, and forsake wrath! Fret not yourself; it tends only to evil."

How I want to "refrain from anger"! I desperately want to "forsake wrath." I'm so tired of the chain of events that happens when I'm angry. Either I plunge into a funk of silent brooding, or I hurt people I love and care about with my outbursts.

Verse 7 of Psalm 37 seems like an answer to my prayer from yesterday: "Be still before the Lord and wait patiently for Him; fret not yourself over the one who prospers in his way, over the man who carries out evil devices!"

I don't have to fret or worry about evil or disobedience having the last word. I don't have to get stressed out when my ways aren't followed. I can be still before You and wait patiently for You. After all, You are Lord of all. You are in control. And You have mercy on me and all people.

Thank You for Your encouragement today, and thank You for letting me trust in You.

Something to think about

Commit your way to the LORD; trust in Him, and He will act.

Psalms 37:5

Fifty Percent

Dear God,

Your listening ear is a blessing to me. I'm so glad I can call upon You when I am troubled. You bless me by paying attention to me. I know You hear my cry.

I've been feeling terribly guilty for blowing up at my son over the weekend. He got home late, didn't clean his room after we asked him, and said a disrespectful "whatever" to his mom when she confronted him about it. That's all it took. I lost it. It wasn't pretty.

No matter how much I vow to myself that I will stay in control, certain things set me off and send me into a downward spiral of fury. I probably shouldn't have been up that late. Being tired doesn't help. I should have stayed out of the argument, but I feel like I need to defend my wife when she is treated poorly.

Sometimes I can get through these situations. Too many other times I fail. I'm living well for about fifty percent of the time.

If only I could stay in the positive fifty percent! But I'm not. And it's causing pain.

I need You to grow me and to be my strength, O Lord. This problem is too big for me. Jesus carried all of my sins and weaknesses as He hung on the cross. Please put to death the anger in me that brings hurt to the people I love. Please bring to life in me a new heart and spirit of patience and peace.

Something to think about

The Lord gives strength to His people; the Lord blesses His people with peace.

Psalm 29:11 NIV

Isolation

Dear God,

In Christ I am a new creation. The old is gone and the new has come. I cling to that Good News and praise You for Your forgiveness and grace. You are good to me. You do not treat me as my sins deserve. Thank You for Your love.

Your attitude toward me is my lifeline right now. I can tell that others in my life have a different attitude. It is one that I caused them to have. There are people who keep their distance from me because of my anger. They think of me as an angry and moody person. They see me as a "time bomb" ready to explode at any moment.

I admit that this perception has been well-founded. At home, at sporting events, at meetings, and even on the phone, I've lost my temper and lashed out with a loud voice and unpleasant words.

But the isolation bothers me. Being treated with kid gloves or having people walk on eggshells all the time makes me even more angry. But what can I do? I've driven people away. I've put fear in their hearts. How do I undo the results of my anger?

Only You can put me on a new path, dear Savior. Only You can lead me to establish a new track record and a new reputation. You could have lashed out at me and destroyed me because of my sin, but instead, You gave Your life for me. Help me to show the love and patience You first showed to me. Help me to reflect the relationship of peace I now have with You.

Something to think about

Therefore, since we have been justified by faith, we have peace with God through our Lord Jesus Christ.

Romans 5:1

My Problem?

Dear God,

I walked out of a meeting yesterday. When I raised objections about some points in the proposed plan, people looked at me as if I was out of my mind. My blood was boiling, so I got up and left. I thought it was better to leave than to start yelling at the hard-headed people in the room.

This is where I'm struggling most as I wrestle with my anger: people provoke me! It doesn't seem to be my problem as much as it is everyone else who pushes me, tests me, and sends me over the edge.

At least that's my first reaction. But I know I am not supposed to look at the speck in my brother's eye until I confront the reality of the log in my own eye. And I do have a big log of anger that gets expressed in many unhealthy ways. My temper flares. I flee confrontations and difficult conversations. I lose sleep as I mull over the frustrating events of the day. I complain to others when I should speak directly to the person involved. I become grouchy and loud.

Please forgive me, God. Please break through the barriers that prevent me from moving forward in a healthy way. I can't do this by myself, but I know that You love me and that, with You, nothing is impossible.

Something to think about

But now in Christ Jesus you who once were far off have been brought near by the blood of Christ. For He Himself is our peace, who has made us both one and has broken down in His flesh the dividing wall of hostility.

Ephesians 2:13–14

I

Dear God,

This hasn't been a good week. Behind closed doors I bawled out a co-worker. But it got bad when he pushed back at some of my complaints about his performance. I started yelling. I threw a clipboard across the room. The impact broke several coffee mugs on a shelf. He left the room looking very frightened.

I lost control. When that happens, I become loud and foul and even profane. I say things I regret. I become mean. This has to stop. I know it's not good for me or anyone else.

After the yelling episode, I searched "Anger Management" on the Internet. The Web site I found was describing me! I know I need to find better ways to express my anger and frustration. I can't bury my feelings, but I can't let them explode, either. Instead of becoming accusatory and aggressive toward others, the Web site advised using "I statements" when expressing anger: "I feel frustrated,"

"I'm disappointed," "I must have been misunderstood."

The biggest "I statement" for me right now is: "I need some help with this." The article said that anger is a natural and healthy emotion, but should be expressed appropriately. Dear God, I've crossed the line and I need You to help me. I know You care about me. Please give me courage to ask for help. Please give me wisdom to follow Your path.

Something to think about

A fool gives full vent to his spirit, but a wise man quietly holds it back.

Proverbs 29:11

An Answer

Dear God,

You really do answer prayers. Thank You for hearing my cry for help. I mess up so often, but You still respond to me with mercy and grace. Thank You for giving me second chances.

Your answer came in the form of someone to talk to and receive counsel from. I asked my pastor if I could meet him for lunch. He agreed. I told him about my struggle with anger. I felt embarrassed, but he let me know that it was normal to have struggles in life. He said that each of us has a weakness or two. That's why we need Jesus.

He told me that getting into new and healthy habits would take some time, but that God could help me right away. My pastor walked me through Psalm 4 in the Bible. Just as the Web site said, my pastor said that anger is an emotion we need, but it needs to be expressed appropriately. Psalm 4 says to express it without sinning. The Psalm also directs us to deliberate in our hearts and minds—silently—before an outward expression takes over. Most important, the Psalm says to do the right thing before God by putting trust in Him.

Those are wise and life-changing words. I think some of my anger happens because I want to control things, but I can't. Thank You, God, for Your Word. It changes my perspective and gives me new life. Thank You for showing me that You are faithful and trustworthy. Help me to trust You and to walk in Your ways.

Something to think about

Be angry, and do not sin; ponder in your own hearts on your beds, and be silent. Offer right sacrifices, and put your trust in the LORD.

Psalms 4:4–5

Mending

Dear God,

It is only because of You that I am living in a new way. Only Your grace and strength bring change in my life. Thank You for helping me.

At work today, I apologized to my co-workers for making them feel intimidated, belittled, and frightened. I also brought a supply of replacement coffee mugs for the ones I broke. A few people chuckled when I showed them the box of new mugs, but I know they don't fully trust me yet. It's okay. I know it will take time.

I also called the counselor my pastor recommended. I'm going to start meeting with him once each week. It sounds like he can help me with my anger. At the very least, it's good to know I'll have someone to talk to on a regular basis. Knowing I'll have a dependable time to vent and process things will help me keep my feelings under control the rest of the week—at least I hope so.

My prayer today, God, is that as You help me mend the relationships I've hurt because of my anger, You will also help mend me inside. I want to stop the control anger has over me. I don't want to get physically violent anymore. I don't want to hold grudges and give people the silent treatment while I boil on the inside. I don't want to hurt anyone—with my words or with my physical outbursts. Please make me new inside and out. I know You can.

Something to think about

Create in me a clean heart, O God, and renew a right spirit within me. Cast me not away from Your presence, and take not Your Holy Spirit from me. Restore to me the joy of Your salvation, and uphold me with a willing spirit.

Psalm 51:10–12

Just Like You

DEAR GOD,

The more I read the Bible, the more I see that I want to be like You. You're the perfect guide to handling anger. You showed that anger is normal. When You were frustrated, such as when people worshiped false gods or turned the temple into a marketplace, You expressed Your anger. But You always did it in the right way at the right time. And You always let Your mercy prevail.

Most of all, You chose not to unleash Your anger on us. Instead, You forgave our sins by letting the full force of Your righteous anger fall upon Your Son, Jesus. You sacrificed Him to save us.

That is a precious gift in my life. Please lead me to share that gift with the people You have placed around me. Instead of spewing anger at everyone, please let Your mercy prevail in me and through me. Help me to sacrifice my own desire to be right or pleased and, instead, be a humble servant to my family, friends, and co-workers.

I really want to be like You, God. Lead me in Your path of righteousness and truth. Lead me in the steps of Your Son, Jesus.

Something to think about

But You, O Lord, are a God merciful and gracious, slow to anger and abounding in steadfast love and faithfulness.

Psalm 86:15

Walking

Dear God,

You are a lamp to my feet and a light to my path. You lead me and direct me to walk the right way. Today, I walked away from a situation that, normally, would have been an angry and explosive encounter. Instead of engaging in it in the heat of the moment, I paused, let people know that we had to think about what was going on for a little while, and walked away.

I could see that people were shocked. They expected me to blow up. But I didn't. I was trembling by the time I got to my office, but after taking a few deep breaths and coming to You in prayer, I calmed down and could think about the situation.

It felt so good not to be controlled by my anger. After the wave of emotion passed, I could actually think clearly about what action to take. Later in the day we met, regrouped, and figured out a solution.

Thank You for rescuing me. Thank You for walking with me and letting me walk with You. Thank You for slowing me down and directing me in a walk of peace and righteousness.

Something to think about

My dear brothers and sisters, take note of this: Everyone should be quick to listen, slow to speak and slow to become angry, because human anger does not produce the righteousness that God desires.

James 1:19–20 NIV

A Future

Dear God,

Your Word and the good counsel You have placed in my life seem to be helping. I have gone from being stuck in anger and having no hope to being able to envision a future of balanced and healthy living. I praise You for your faithful work in my life. Thank You for being my Savior and Friend.

Please know that I am still very weak. I can't rely on my own strength. My experience has shown me that it is much too easy for me to fail. The devil is still prowling around seeking to devour me. Circumstances in life will still provoke me. That's why I'm calling on You.

Please don't abandon me. Please forgive all the times I've failed You and others. And please walk with me in Your strength and peace. I need You to complete what You've started. I like what You are doing in my life. I want to keep growing as a person who honors You in my thoughts, words, and actions. I don't want to slip back into temper fits that are laced with profanity and blind rage.

Thank You for loving me, O Lord. Keep me steady in Your care. Grant me a future with You.

Something to think about

Mark the blameless and behold the upright, for there is a future for the man of peace.

Psalm 37:37

Never Solo

Dear God,

Every day I realize more and more that we are not meant to live life as solo acts. You've opened my eyes to that. In my anger, I felt that it was always me against the world—me against inefficient co-workers, me against rebellious kids, me against a contrary spouse, and me against the church council—I think You get the idea.

But now I see that I was being self-centered and proud. Instead of believing that other people have answers and solutions, I felt I was the only one. Instead of consulting people for opinions, I jumped to my own conclusions. Instead of listening and seeking to understand, I barged in with what I wanted to say. I was wrong and arrogant for believing that everyone was below me. Please forgive me for my pride.

Now I know that You are with me. When I

received communion the other day in church, I was truly moved by Your commitment to dwell in me and make me a new creation in Christ. Your Word has been a companion that balances me and strengthens me. The counselor You've provided has been a refuge for my disturbed soul and a source of accountability as I deliberate my words and actions.

I know it will still take some time to live consistently in service to You and others. I realize that I will have to be patient as people learn to trust me again. But through it all I know that I do not walk alone. Thank You.

Something to think about

"For the mountains may depart and the hills be removed, but My steadfast love shall not depart from you, and My covenant of peace shall not be removed," says the Lord, who has compassion on you.

Isaiah 54:10

A Good Day

Dear God,

Today was a good day. Thank You for the gift of a day in which I could communicate calmly and effectively with everyone around me and in which I felt no fury bubbling up from within. It's not that everything went right today. It's just that You filled me with peace that I couldn't even understand. You stood guard over my heart and mind. I praise You for Your faithful work in my life.

Honestly, I didn't expect this kind of day so soon. I felt like my anger was an issue that would take years of struggling to overcome. My outbursts seemed too big and too complex to be able to experience any sign of progress in a short period of time.

But now I see that my serious issues are very manageable for You. What is vast and overwhelming to me is easy for You to handle. What I keep forgetting is that You are God and I'm not. I am not only a sinner in my actions, but also in my perception of the problems and obstacles I face. I make You too small and my problems too big. Thank You for rescuing me from that hopelessness.

Your Son's death for me paid the price for my errors and misdeeds. Jesus carried the consequences of my sins to the cross. Now I have been blessed with the gift of new life with Him. Thank You for not making me wait years to see that today can be a good day.

Something to think about

But He was pierced for our transgressions; He was crushed for our iniquities; upon Him was the chastisement that brought us peace, and with His wounds we are healed.

Isaiah 53:5

What's Important

Dear God,

It is not an easy thing navigating this journey with anger when people around me know what buttons to push. I may be on this new path willingly, but the people driving on the roads, the rude person at the store, and even my kids aren't necessarily being careful not to make me angry. This is challenging.

But You've shown me what is truly important in life. I am not here to insist on my happiness or comfort—even though I feel that way sometimes. I am here to serve You and to show Your love to Your people. Whether it is a stranger or a family member, it's not all about me.

This has been a challenging lesson. I want to be right. I don't want people to get away with things. I don't want to feel insulted or slighted. But even as You suffered for me, I know that it is an honor to suffer for Your glory. I have to swallow a lot of pride and hold back a good number of words, but I want to excel in what is important. Please help me do that.

It's good to know that I don't have to bottle up my anger. I can talk with my counselor every week. I can refrain from outbursts and process it in prayer and conversation later.

The outcome is a blessing. For the first time in a long time, I am helping to create environments free from strife. At home, at work, and even when I am on my own, I help cultivate peace instead of trouble. You are my strength, O Lord! Keep it up! Please!

Something to think about

Better is a dry morsel with quiet than a house full of feasting with strife.

Proverbs 17:1

Delighting

Dear God,

Over the past weeks, I've realized that I used to delight in powering up and showing some wrath—at least there was a part of me that felt that way. I liked to exert forceful control. I didn't mind when I frightened someone into submission. But now I see that I want to delight in what You do: showing mercy and creating peace.

It doesn't mean I want to be a wimp. I know I still need to stand up for what is right, defend the least of these, and protect those in danger. I know I still need to be strong. But I'm learning to exercise strength in a patient and appropriate way. Thank You for leading me. Thank You for changing my heart.

I also see that I can't control other people. I'm not supposed to control other people. I can influence others. I can work with people. I can teach and, in some cases, discipline others. But my job is not to control. That's Your job.

Help me to trust in You, to rely on Your help, and to remain Your servant. Lead me to delight in reflecting Your heart to everyone around me. Help me discover a new kind of strength in You.

Something to think about

Who is a God like You, who pardons sin and forgives the transgression of the remnant of His inheritance? You do not stay angry forever but delight to show mercy.

Micah 7:18 NIV

Reflection

Dear God,

All did not go perfectly today. I was tired. Honestly, I was grouchy. I snapped at a few people and had an ugly argument with one of my kids. Fortunately, my wife helped me walk away from what could have been a lot worse.

Today was a reminder that I am not perfect and that anger is a constant weakness in my life. This will continue to be a moment-to-moment and day-to-day challenge.

But I thank and praise You for the victories You have brought into my life so far. I give thanks to You that I can lean on Your forgiveness and strength when I fail. After another round of apologies, I will start brand new. I will not lose hope. I know You fight for me. I know You gave Your Son for me. I know that He is alive and well, interceding for me at Your right hand.

Please continue to shape my character to be like Yours. Please lead me to be slow to anger, filled with grace, and ready to show love in all circumstances. I want to be a person who is a reflection of You.

Something to think about

But You, O Lord, are a God merciful and gracious, slow to anger and abounding in steadfast love and faithfulness.

Psalm 86:15

Bearing Fruit

Dear God,

You are good. Your love endures forever. I see evidence of Your love in my life. You care about me enough to expose my weaknesses and lead me to face them and deal with them. You treasure me so much that you refuse to let me become stagnant in life. Instead, You keep growing me both with discipline and with blessing.

I admit that I am not always a willing student. I'm definitely not worthy of Your love and attention. But You are with me every day. You are committed to my life. You care for me with an everlasting love.

Thank You for Your interest in my life. Thank You for not leaving me in a toxic pool of anger and conflict. Thank You for lifting me out of the pit of wrath and placing me on new and hopeful ground.

I realize now that You are calling me not only to leave a life of uncontrolled and sinful anger, but to grow as a new person. You want me to bear fruit that will last. Your Holy Spirit develops new qualities in me like self-control, patience, gentleness, and peace. Please keep producing this fruit in my life. Grow me as your new creation.

Something to think about

But the fruit of the Spirit is love, joy, peace, patience, kindness, goodness, faithfulness, gentleness, self-control; against such things there is no law.

Galatians 5:22–23

New Firsts

Dear God,

In the past, my first reaction was to immediately respond to anything that provoked me. My default was to power up or to withdraw—making it obvious that I could argue or freeze someone out with the best of them. Now I know these are unhealthy actions. You've taught me that. You have graciously stepped into my life and showed me a new way, a way of peace.

Thank You for leading me to practice a new set of first reactions. You've shown me that I don't need to sin when I am angry. I can be quiet and consult You in prayer. You've shown me that instead of veering into wrong and hurtful outbursts, I can follow Your Word and guidance by serving others at all times. You've shown me that instead of holding a simmering grudge, I can speak the truth in love and solve a conflict with someone. You've shown me that I am not running my life. I am not in charge.

You lead me and You will help me no matter how deep the valley or challenging the incline.

You are teaching me to trust You—even in my struggle with anger.

Stay with me, dear Savior. Keep leading me. Continue to pour Your strength into me. I know I am Your baptized and redeemed child. Please lead me to excel in new firsts as I depend upon You and grow in Your grace and truth.

Something to think about

You keep him in perfect peace whose mind is stayed on You, because he trusts in You.

Isaiah 26:3

General Prayers

Lord's Prayer

Our Father, who art in heaven, hallowed be Thy name, Thy kingdom come, Thy will be done on earth as it is in heaven. Give us this day our daily bread; and forgive us our trespasses as we forgive those who trespass against us; and lead us not into temptation, but deliver us from evil. For Thine is the kingdom and the power and the glory forever and ever. Amen.

Morning Prayer

I thank You, my heavenly Father, through Jesus Christ, Your dear Son, that You have kept me this night from all harm and danger; and I pray that You would keep me this day also from sin and every evil, that all my doings and life may please You. For into Your hands I commend myself, my body and soul, and all things. Let Your holy angel be with me, that the evil foe may have no power over me. Amen.

Evening Prayer

I thank You, my heavenly Father, through Jesus Christ, Your dear Son, that You have graciously kept me this day; and I pray that You would forgive me all my sins where I have done wrong, and graciously keep me this night. For into Your hands I commend myself, my body and soul, and all things. Let Your holy angel be with me, that the evil foe may have no power over me. Amen.

For Patience

O God, by the patient endurance of Your only-begotten Son You beat down the pride of the old enemy. Help us to treasure rightly in our hearts what our Lord has borne for our sakes that, after His example, we may bear with patience those things that are adverse to us; through Jesus Christ, our Lord. Amen. (*LSB*, p. 312)

For Forgiveness

Lord God, You have given me another day, a day to live in Your service and for the good of my fellowmen. I am indeed a poor tool in Your hand and deserving to be cast aside. Forgive me all my sins for Jesus' sake, and by Your Spirit grant me the fitness to work for You this day. I beseech You to make me mindful, dear Lord, that I am but a stranger and a pilgrim in this present world. Let me not devote my efforts today to purposes unworthy of You; let me not gather treasures merely for this world; let me not serve mammon. This life is but a vain show; let me not search for an abiding city here. But, Lord, fasten my heart and hope on the life that is in You, and let my strivings and desires be directed to the treasures of Your love. As long as I am in the land of my pilgrimage, hold my hand, Lord; keep me from every straying path. If I should stumble in sinful weakness, grant me repentance and faith; for Jesus' sake. Amen. (*Lutheran Book of Prayer*, p. 34)

Suggested Scripture Readings

Whoever is slow to anger is better than the mighty, and he who rules his spirit than he who takes a city.

Proverbs 16:32

Return to the Lord your God, for He is gracious and merciful, slow to anger, and abounding in steadfast love.

Joel 2:13

I call upon You, for You will answer me, O God; incline Your ear to me; hear my words.

Psalm 17:6

The Lord redeems the life of His servants; none of those who take refuge in Him will be condemned.

Psalm 34:22

Aim for restoration, comfort one another, agree with one another, live in peace; and the

God of love and peace will be with you. . . . The grace of the Lord Jesus Christ and the love of God and the fellowship of the Holy Spirit be with you all.

2 Corinthians 13:11–14

And above all these put on love, which binds everything together in perfect harmony. And let the peace of Christ rule in your hearts, to which indeed you were called in one body. And be thankful. Let the word of Christ dwell in you richly, teaching and admonishing one another in all wisdom, singing psalms and hymns and spiritual songs, with thankfulness in your hearts to God.

Colossians 3:14–16

Let your speech always be gracious, seasoned with salt, so that you may know how you ought to answer each person.

Colossians 4:6